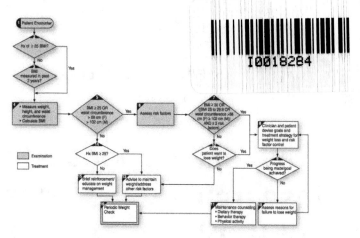

* This algorithm applies only to the assessment for overweight and obesity and subsequent decisions based on that assessment. It does not include any initial overall assessment for cardiovascular risk factors or diseases that are indicated.

Algorithms

by:netanel stern

Table Of Contents:

Why did I choose to research this subject? 3

What is an Algorithm? 3

Why do we use algorithms? 3

What is a euclid's algorithm? 4

When should you use the Euclid's Algorithm? 4

what it's dijkstra algorithm? 5

how to use in dijkstra algorithm? 5

when need to using in dijkstra algorithm? 5

what it's pseudocode? 5

what it's the time complexity? 6

what it's Space Complexity? 7

what it's greedy algorithm? 7

what it's turing machine? 8

Bibliography: 8

further reading/watch: 9

Reflection: 9

Why did I choose to research this subject?

I chose to research this subject because I am interested in computer science. the Computer science field is developing most rapidly and it is a "hot" field today.

What is an Algorithm?

An Algorithm is a sequence of steps that solve a mathematical problem. A precise step-by-step plan for a computational procedure that possibly begins with an input value and ends with an output value in a finite number of steps.[1]

Why do we use algorithms?

An algorithm is a sequence of operations

_____

[1] "algorithm - Wiktionary." https://en.wiktionary.org/wiki/algorithm .תאריך גישה: 17 ינו׳. 2017.

that can be carried out "mechanically"and

does not require intelligent human intervention at any point. Not all algorithms are computer programs, but any algorithm can be implemented as a computer program. Conversely, every computer program is an algorithm. To cut a long story short, algorithms are everywhere.[2]

What is a euclid's algorithm?

Euclid's Algorithm is a way for finding the greatest common divisor of two numbers a and b.[3]

Why
.https://www.qu

Euclidean Algori
.http://mathworld.wc

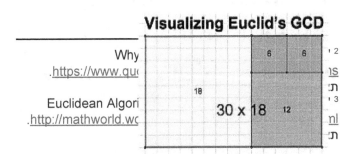

Visualizing Euclid's GCD

30 x 18

When should you use the Euclid's Algorithm?

Euclid algorithm is used when you want to find the greatest common divisor. Advanced algorithms factoring algorithm using it. In addition, this algorithm is considered the most ancient algorithm because it has already appeared in the book "Elements" by Euclid.

what it's dijkstra algorithm?

Dijkstra's algorithm is an algorithm for finding the shortest paths between nodes in a **weighted graph**[4] [5].

---

[4] A graph is a pictorial representation of a set of objects where some pairs of objects are connected by links.

how to use in dijkstra algorithm?

the dijkstra algorithm accepts as input **weighted graph** and outputs the shortest lane between node a to node b.

Dijkstra's algorithm - Wikipedia."" [5]
תאריך .https://en.wikipedia.org/wiki/Dijkstra's_algorithm
גישה: 17 ינו׳. 2017.

when need to using in dijkstra algorithm?

GPS navigation device should use Dijkstra algorithm to navigate because for any arc have value (in this case This is distance).

what it's pseudocode?

Pseudocode is an informal high-level description of the

operating principle of a computer program or other algorithm.[6] pseudocode can be written in many ways but it's usually written by the rules of Any programming language or this syntax[7]:

pseudocode standard	visual basic
READ height of rectangle READ width of rectangle COMPUTE area as height times width	dim height as integer dim width as integer dim area as integer = height * width

---

[6] "Pseudocode - Wikipedia. https://en.wikipedia.org/wiki/Pseudocode תאריך גישה: 17 ינו'. 2017.

[7] By comparison is shown functionally identical syntax in the programming language Visual Basic

what it's the time complexity?

In computer science, the time complexity of an algorithm quantifies the amount of time taken by an algorithm to run as a function of the length of the string representing the input.[8] For an example, the

_____

[8] Time complexity - Wikipedia."" https://en.wikipedia.org/wiki/Time_complexity. תאריך גישה: 31 ינו'. 2017.

Attached LINK
https://en.wikipedia.org/wiki/Computational_complexity_of_mathematical_operations

time complexity of euclid's algorithm is logarithmic in the worst case[9] and therefore is directly proportional to the number of digits.

However Dijkstra algorithm's time complexity is O(s*|E|log|E|+|V|).

Euclidean Algorithm -- from Wolfram MathWorld.""[9]
.http://mathworld.wolfram.com/EuclideanAlgorithm.html
.2017 תאריך גישה: 1 פבר׳.

what it's Space Complexity?

The way in which the amount of storage space required by an algorithm varies with the size of the problem it is solving. Space complexity is normally expressed as an order of magnitude, e.g.[10]

---

for example [10]

$O(N^2)$ means that if the size of the problem (N) doubles then four times as much working storage will be needed. [11] in addition, time complexity of the euclid algorithm it's $O(1)$ that means constant space

_____

Space complexity | Define Space complexity at" [11] Dictionary.com."

.http://www.dictionary.com/browse/space-complexity

תאריך גישה: 15 פברי. 2017.

on memory[12]. However Dijkstra algorithm's space complexity is $O(\mathbf{V}^2)$.

what it's greedy algorithm?

A greedy algorithm is a mathematical process that looks for simple, easy-to-implement solutions to complex,

[12] "Euclid's Algorithm for GCD Space Complexity - Stack Overflow." 25 מרץ. 2016,
http://stackoverflow.com/questions/36228916/euclids-algorithm-for-gcd-space-complexity. תאריך גישה: 7 פבר׳. 2017.

multi-step problems by deciding which next step will provide the most obvious benefit.[13]

what it's turing machine?

Turing machine is a term from <u>computer science</u>. A Turing machine is a system of rules, states and

[13] What is greedy algorithm? - Definition from" WhatIs.com." <u>http://whatis.techtarget.com/definition/greedy-algorithm</u>. תאריך גישה: 15 פברי. 2017.

transitions rather than a real machine. It was first described by [Alan Turing](). There are two purposes of a Turing machine. Either it can be used to [decide]() [a]() formal [language]() or it solves [mathematical functions](). Turing machines are one of the most important formal models in the study of computer science.[14]

You are welcome to watch the simulation on deutronomistic turing machine for gcd(B10010000,B0101 0111):gcd(144,87).

Bibliography:

- "algorithm - Wiktionary."

---

[14] "Turing machine - Simple English Wikipedia, the free encyclopedia."
https://simple.wikipedia.org/wiki/Turing_machine תאריך. גישה: 8 פבר׳. 2017.

https://en.wiktionary.org/wiki/algorithm.

- "Why do we use algorithms? - Quora." https://www.quora.com/Why-do-we-use-algorithms.

- "Euclidean Algorithm -- from Wolfram MathWorld." http://mathworld.wolfram.com/EuclideanAlgorithm.html.

- "Dijkstra's algorithm - Wikipedia." https://en.wikipedia.org/wiki/Dijkstra's_algorithm.
- "Pseudocode - Wikipedia." https://en.wikipedia.org/wiki/Pseudocode.
- Time complexity - Wikipedia." https://en.wikipedia.org/wiki/Time_complexity

- "Euclidean Algorithm -- from Wolfram MathWorld." http://mathworld.wolfram.com/EuclideanAlgorithm.html.
- Space complexity | Define Space complexity at Dictionary.com." http://www.dictionary.com/browse/space-complexity.
- Euclid's Algorithm for GCD Space

Complexity - Stack Overflow." http://stackoverflow.com/questions/36228916/euclids-algorithm-for-gcd-space-complexity.

- "What is greedy algorithm? - Definition from WhatIs.com." http://whatis.techtarget.com/definition/greedy-algorithm.

- "Turing machine - Simple English

Wikipedia, the free encyclopedia."
https://simple.wikipedia.org/wiki/Turing_machine

further reading/watch:

- *Cormen, Thomas, Charles Leiserson,*

Ronald Rivest, and Clifford Stein. [Introduction to Algorithms](#).

- [dijkstra algorithm (video)](#)

Reflection:

I reviewed many topics in the field of computer science. Computer science is evolving all the time. Please note that this is a discipline that many people fail And don't forget the next proverb: "I've missed over 9,000 shots in my career. I've lost almost 300 games. 26 times I've been trusted to take the game-winning shot and missed. I've failed over and over and over again in my life. And that is why I succeed."(michael jordan). In addition I'm sure this article will interest you on your part to continue to study computer science.

www.ingramcontent.com/pod-product-compliance
Lightning Source LLC
LaVergne TN
LVHW052126070326
832902LV00038B/3971